The Journey To Peace

The Journey To Peace

K. ENGLISH

Rock of Ages Publishing
412 N Main St Suite 100
Buffalo, Wyoming 82834

Rock of Ages Publishing
412 Main St. Suite 100
Buffalo, Wyoming 82834
www.roapublishing.com

Library of Congress Control Number: 2016903981

For additional information or group sales please contact the publisher at the address above.

ISBN 978-0-9897554-0-5

First Edition
Printed in the United States of America
14 13 12 11 10 RZE 10 9 8 7 6 5 4 3 2 1

I am grateful and thankful to God for leading me on such an incredible Journey to Peace

I wish to personally thank my loving wife for her contributions to my inspiration and knowledge and other help in creating this book

This book is dedicated to the memory

of

Mary Inez Johnson

Contents

Introduction

Does God Exist? – *Prove It!*

I Want to Meet God – *I Can't Even See Him, Where Do I Begin?*

Waiting on God – *Always How Long Will This Take?*

Frustrated with God – *I'm Not Hanging Around Here Forever!*

It's Not My Fault – *Well Don't Look at Me I Didn't Do It!*

Struggling with Submission – *Submit! Are You Kidding Me!*

Identify Yourself – *I Know Who I Am*

Taking The Next Step – *No Thanks! I'm Comfortable Right Here*

Moving Forward – *Hold On, Not So Fast I'm Not Ready*

The Days Ahead – *Wait a Minute, I Should Expect What?*

Learning to Trust God – *Trust is Something You Earn Not Learn*

A Wise Decision – *That Remains to Be Seen*

Discover Your Life – *Uh, Hello! It Wasn't Lost*

Balancing Life – *Not a Problem I'm Great at Multi-Tasking*

Consider Your Focus – *I Have This Whole Thing Remains Blurry*

You Can Say No – *Gee Thanks After All It Is My Life*

A New Life to Share – *I Never Share, Please Stay in Your Lane*

Contents

Worship My Way — *No Thank You I'm Good, You Do You*

Let Go — *Of What? I'm Not Holding Anything*

What is Reality — *This Is What I've Been Asking All Along*

Live in His Moment — *I'm Too Busy Trying to Live in My Own*

Make Your Life Real Today —*My Life Is as Real as It Gets*

Notes

Bibliography

Introduction

Where there is true faith, it will challenge every logical concept of the world as we know it while bringing eternity to the present. This book is not a study of religion, science, theology, nor is it about astrology or any type of spiritual mysticism. This is a book of discovery, a roadmap for a relational journey.

We all feel something is missing. We can never be satisfied we always want more, no matter how much we possess, it never seems to be enough. What we do know or at least believe is our existence. Man undoubtedly has a very definite reality we know we exist it's obvious. Our life is purely physical a level of limited observation because the awareness of the physical is merely our perception, and even that comes with an extremely limited level of understanding. Despite this revelation, everyone remains a mystery unto themselves searching for transcendent comfort. As humans we are certainly not what we physically appear to be, we desire to live longer, be healthier, look younger all the while wanting, almost needing more.

The faith-driven person will speak to the condition of the hearer; otherwise, they speak a language known only to themselves. The message must be timeless yet timely. Each written word must communicate to every generation. The message of this book is not born out of our modern times and can be applied to all generations. It is written due to a lack of faith which has been empty for years and is steadily growing worse. The primary problem is an insignificant view of God. Modern Christianity no longer produces people who can appreciate or experience life in the Spirit. We regularly forfeit our spirit of worship by choosing the fiction of our world further paralyzing our ability to escape inwardly to meet God in doting silence. When we hear or read, words like "Be still, and know that I am God," they have absolutely no meaning to the self-confident, hurried worshipper in this modern age. It is more than obvious when we understand there are not many people breaking down doors to get to the many books on religious subject matter available today. After all, why should we, these types of books are not as impressive as the modern day secular masterpieces that so many are so impulsively drawn towards.

It is not a wonder that it has become all but impossible to maintain our moral practices and keep our inner attitudes in check while our idea of God is erroneous or inadequate. When you consider most people are not the slightest bit concerned about, or conscious of the existence of a creator, and in many instances have traded the notion altogether for their own personal God. If we want to actually experience peace in our lives, we must think of God as He is.

I have written these pages as my modest contribution to not only this generation, but generations to come. For your consideration, I humbly offer these simple writings of the Journey to Peace.

Since this book is neither theological nor technical, and since it is written in an easy to understand everyday language with no pretense to some elegant literary style, perhaps some will be drawn to read it. There is nothing here that would be contrary to sound Christian theology. However, it is not written for approval. Not from the theologians, Christians, or any of the many religious groups or organizations that exist, it was not even written for the endorsement of faithful church-goers. No, this book is written for the ordinary everyday person whose heart stirs within to seek after God Himself. I hope this small book will somehow contribute to the promotion of personal growth and heart relationships, and if but a few people reading it are encouraged to begin their own journey and start the practice of reverent meditation on knowing the very being of God, that will more than satisfy its intent.

Does God Exist?
Prove It!

"The heavens declare the glory of God, and the sky above proclaims his handiwork." - Psalms 19:1

Look around at the extraordinary and beautiful things of nature. Think of their awe-inspiring adaptation to the needs and happiness, of all living creatures. The sunshine and the rain that delight and refresh the earth, the hills, seas, and plains, all speak to us of a Creator's love. It is impossible to positively prove or definitively disprove the existence of God. That does not mean, however, that there is no evidence of God's existence. There is more to the question "is there a God?" than pure intellectual concerns.

Those who probe into the rational arguments for and against the Creator will soon discover that there is seemingly never an end to this debate. For every argument made in support of God's existence, there is a cynic who poses another in direct dispute of that existence. One must first realize that human reasoning is not the best way to determine whether God exists or not. There is arguably a type of knowledge that is not reasoned out in the human mind, wisdom that does not come from mere observation and experience. God purposely left the door ajar to the human psyche for both faith and doubt. Everyone must choose whether to trust in God or to believe only in what they resolve through human reasoning. To those who choose to believe in God and seek Him, God reveals

Himself. To those who choose not to believe, God remains nothing more than a fable.

People claim to reject God's existence because it is "not scientific" or "because there is no logical proof." The truth is that once they admit that there is a God, they also must realize that they are responsible and accountable to God. There is an abundance of reasons to believe in God; yet, the real question remains whether or not the person is open to exploring the evidence. It takes humility to accept that we cannot figure everything out on our own. Most would agree that no matter how we all arrived here it was because of something much bigger than we are; therefore limited human reasoning is not the best way to determine whether an infinite God exists. God allows Himself to be discovered to those who become as "babies" while hiding Himself in the shroud of darkness from the wise and the prudent. The Bible tells us in the book of Psalm 19:1-4 "The heavens declare the glory of God; the skies proclaim the work of His hands. Day, after day, they pour forth speech; night after night they display knowledge. There is no speech or language where their voice is not heard. Their voice goes out into all the earth, their words to the ends of the world". Looking at the stars, understanding the vastness of the universe, observing the wonders of nature, seeing the beauty of a sunset—all of these things point to a Creator no other than God.

If this were not enough, there is also evidence of God in our hearts. The book of Ecclesiastes 3:11 tells us, "...He has also set eternity in the hearts of men." God has bound us to Him placing the desire to know Him in the form of eternity in our hearts. Deep within us is the recognition that there is something beyond this life and this world. We can deny this knowledge intellectually, but God's presence in us and all around us is still very apparent. You will find the path to Him through the things of nature, and also, in the deepest earthly ties that human hearts can know, through it all He has sought to reveal Himself to us. All of the imperfect things of the world perfectly represent His love for us.

The Bible also proclaims that people are without excuse for not believing in God. "For since the creation of the world God's invisible qualities. His eternal power and divine nature have been clearly seen, being understood from what has been made, so that men are without excuse" Romans 1:20. Despite this, the Bible warns that some will still deny God's existence: In Psalm 14:1 "The fool says in his heart, 'There is no God." The Bible also tells us that people will reject the clear and undeniable knowledge of God and believe a lie instead. Romans 1:25, "They exchanged the truth of God for a lie and worshiped and served created things rather than the Creator.

People will reject God's existence because there is no proof tangible enough for them. The fact is simply, if God exists, then we are all accountable to Him for our actions. If God does not exist, then we can do whatever we want, when we want without having to worry about the consequences. That is why many of those who deny the existence of God cling firmly to the theory of naturalistic evolution—it gives them an alternative to believing in a scientific creation rather than a Creator.

Since the vast majority of people throughout history, in all cultures, from all civilizations, and on all continents throughout the world believe in the existence of some God. It is safe to say there must be something or someone causing this belief. God exists, and ultimately everyone knows He exists. The very fact that some attempt aggressively to disprove His existence is, in fact, an argument for His existence.

God has put an urge inside of every one of us, an insatiable craving, an unquenchable thirst, it is the compulsion to seek Him. "No man can come to me," said our Lord, "except the Father, which hath sent me draw him." It is by this predetermined drawing that God takes from us every modicum of credit for the act of our searching. The impulse to pursue God originates with God, but the outworking of that impulse is our deliberate quest after Him, and all the time we are trying to determine whether we are able to prove He exist or to disprove His existence, we are ultimately seeking Him.

Our shady habit of seeking God for no reason other than to prove or disprove His existence effectively prevents us from finding God in full revelation. If we could only omit the "if" in our search, we shall soon find God, only in Him shall we find our genuine selves which is without a doubt our most secret longing.

Our commitment must be sincere so to simplify our approach to Him. We must put away all effort to amaze, and come with the straightforward truthfulness of our youth. If we do this, without a doubt, God who is always ever so near will quickly respond. The Bible says that we must accept by faith the fact that God exists: "Without faith it is impossible to please God. Anyone who comes to Him must believe that He exists and that He rewards those who earnestly seek Him" Hebrews 11:6. If God so desired, He could simply appear and prove to the entire world that He exists. But if He did that, there would be no need for faith. "Then Jesus told him because you have seen me, you have believed; blessed are those who have not seen and yet have believed" John 20:29.

So, does God exist? There is no argument convincing enough to persuade anyone who refuses to acknowledge that which is already evident. At the end of the day, if you want to encounter the true and living God, you will find His existence revealed through your faith. Having faith in God is not a blind trip into some black hole; it is a safe walk along warm, bright and sunny shores where many are already standing.

I Want to Meet God
I Can't Even See Him, Where Do I Begin?

"If ye had known me, ye should have known my Father also: and from henceforth ye know him and have seen him... - John 14:7-9

To most people God is an interpretation, not a reality. He is a supposition from evidence which they may even consider somewhat acceptable. There are others who only know of God, never interested enough to give the notion any thought beyond what they may have heard about Him from others. Still to others God is nothing more than an idea, another way to describe goodness or splendor. To those who desire to know Him, He is Law, Life, or Love the creative architect behind the design and wonders of all that exist, yet He remains personally unknown even to those who desire to know Him. The fact is the possibility of an intimate relationship with Him has not even crossed their minds. While conceding His existence, they do not think of Him as fathomable in the tangible sense that we know things or people.

Our trouble is that we think of the visible world as real and doubt the reality of any other. Although there is no denying the existence of the spiritual world, we doubt that it is ever genuine in our accepted meaning of the word "real." Conversely, we know that the world we live in is real.

It is boisterous, insistent and self-demonstrating it does not appeal to our faith; it is here, in our face always beating on our senses to be seen demanding to be accepted as real and final. But the lens of our hearts is so clouded that we cannot see the other reality, shining all around us.

There was a young child who went in search of this other reality because he wanted to meet God. The child didn't know where to go or even where to begin. He only knew God lived very far away, so with his mobile phone in hand and the backpack full of snacks he threw over his shoulder the child began his journey to meet God.

After walking a few blocks, he came across an old man in a nearby park sitting on a bench looking out at the pond feeding the birds. He approached the man offering him snacks and juice; the old man graciously accepted, smiled and inquired of the young man where he was going with all those snacks. The young man responded I'm on my way to meet God! The old man looked at the young man with a broad smile so big, and teeth as white as a fresh winter's snow. The young man begins laughing too and decided to take a break from his journey to rest. As the young man sat there with the man together eating snacks and drinking juice, he began drawing pictures.

The old man finished his snacks thanked the young man, took a look over at his picture and asked what he was drawing. "God" was the reply from the young man. The old man's grin grew even wider than before "No one knows what God looks like" the old man said with a polite chuckle. "Oh, but they will in a minute "the boy exclaimed with such excitement as he offered the old man a few more snacks, and once again the old man beamed with delight.

Far too often we have preconceived notions as to who God is or isn't and, therefore, miss seeing Him in the moment. Just like the young child, Jesus calls us into meeting God for the first time by sending us on a journey of trust, with the faith to dive in and know Him in the "now." Meeting God is not something you can learn how to do. It's a real-time revelation that comes by Gods Spirit. Knowing God is not the same as understanding arithmetic, philosophy, or even nuclear science, knowing Him is not something you just recall based on memorization. God is NOW type of immediate experience. Knowing God requires meeting Him today in the here and now.

After spending the day in the park eating, drawing, and watching the man smile. Observing as he nodded and often exchange pleasantries with nearly every passerby while birds filled the air with song and butterflies danced to the melodies. The young man rose up shook the old man's hand and begin to walk back toward the direction he first appeared. "Hey I thought you were going to meet God?" to which the boy quickly responded but I did. Now I'm going home, the old man smiled, then looking down noticed the young man had forgotten his pictures. Hey, wait you forgot your pictures of God. The young man turned and replied you keep them I already know what God looks like, the man again smiled, chuckled and bid the young man farewell. When the young man got home he excitedly ran into the house out of breath, his mother inquired where he had been all day. He told his mom, I met God and spent the whole day with Him, He has the most beautiful smile.

If we could all only become like little children, letting go of everything, we can see Him in the now. We could meet Him even now. Unfortunately, too many times the way we remember God depends on how He has been presented to us. We tend to remember Him precisely as He has always been described to us, or how He has always appeared to us in a dream or alone in our imagination. We limit ourselves and God by placing Him in a box where we can only imagine our encounter with the Almighty would be similar if not exactly the way we have always imagined Him to be. As a result, we miss Him even though He is never far from anyone of us we simply can't see God.

Imagine getting to meet with the Almighty, the Creator of the universe the One, who spoke worlds into existence, the One, who breathed and life was born. Unfortunately, this is not how we often think of our heavenly Father. We are usually more aware of our issues, or our present circumstances that have become bigger in our eyes, in our life, greater than God. When in reality we should be blown away that God is already waiting for us.

He speaks to us through his word, through our lives, through life around us. He reminds us of his faithfulness in spite of our faithlessness, He encourages and strengthens our hearts, and continues to reveal more of His glory in spite of our ineptness. If you have never met someone, never seen them, never heard their voice, how would you know them, better still how do you know you haven't already met them?

If you have never met God, and would like to meet Him, the soul has eyes with which to see, perhaps you could take a look at the picture a young child may have left for you. Maybe you could take time with a stranger, or possibly stop and listen to the sounds of life while taking in the wonders of nature all around you.

It's possible you have done one if not all of these things and more yet you are certain you have never met God. Maybe you have, and just didn't recognize Him, well rest assured in knowing you may have missed Him, He surely knew you.

Waiting on God
Always, How Long Will This Take?

"The Lord is good unto them that wait for him, to the soul that seeketh him." - Lamentations 3:25

Every day of your life you find yourself spending time waiting for something. Every one of us has been there whether it is a job interview, waiting for the restroom, the start of a movie, a custom drink from your local Starbucks, or a medical test, in most cases you find, you have no other choice but to wait. If you are anything like me, you too find times when you simply despise waiting. You dislike it so much that sometimes you cannot stop yourself from screaming and cursing on the inside when inconvenienced even if it is only for a moment. Whether you are placed on hold when you call a business, sitting in the waiting room of your doctor's office, or standing in line at the grocery store, like most people in society it is not long before finally realizing how impatient you are.

Nothing challenges your patience more than an attack on your faith because of waiting on God for answers to your prayers. However, waiting is not necessarily a bad thing, waiting reaffirms your dependence on Him as the Authority in your life. When you release the hand of God and run ahead, you are subject to be painfully chastened by the consequences of your own actions resulting in turmoil, exhaustion, and inevitable failure. Waiting on God is an indication that your life is under God's umbrella of power and direction. What can we learn about the art of waiting?

"Are we there yet?" usually these words can be heard coming from the mouths of children whether the wait is five minutes or five hours. However, when time seems to evolve into eternity, even adults begin to pose the same question. Let's take a look at how one might wait to arrive at their destination while traveling. The flight from the Los Angeles International Airport to Singapore is approximately 9,500 miles and takes upwards of 18-and-a-half hours to complete nonstop one-way. This is an incredibly long flight and waiting to arrive at your destination can seem much longer if you are not waiting in the right way. You can just sit and wait and stare at the seat in front of you, which I promise you will make the 18 plus hours seem like an eternity. On the other hand, you can wait engaged in something.

Maybe you have been praying about a situation in your life and now find yourself waiting for a revelation. Sometimes we pray long and hard about a situation in our life without seemingly receiving any answers. Nevertheless, you are troubled so you go on wondering if and when God will answer your prayers if ever at all. We all must wait for answers in life sometimes; nobody can escape the wait. Therefore, the question is not if, but rather how, and how long we will wait.

Some will wait while wondering if something good will happen this is the person just sitting around waiting to see if something happens at all, staring at the back of the seat on the plane doing nothing. This person just sits and waits, and after a very short time of waiting, they get restless and want, what they want, and they want it now. When it does not happen on their time schedule, on their terms, and they feel they have waited, long enough they just give up, saying, "That's it! I've waited and waited forever and nothing's happened." Give me a parachute I have better things to do with my life than sit here and hold on, I'm out. This narcissistic person does not take advantage of time, so for them, waiting is nothing more than a waste of their time.

The humbly submitted person, on the other hand, is expecting, is hopeful, believing the answer is just on the horizon, due to arrive any minute, and on time. Their belief is not a selfish thing. Their heart is full of hope, knowing the problem will be resolved any moment. This person wakes every morning seeking to do something for God. We find some similarities to a humble expectant person and a pregnant woman; we say she is expecting. She has inside her the promise of a baby, and even though she is unable to see the baby, she knows it is there. When she learns she is pregnant, the planning begins, shopping, having baby showers, decorating the nursery, she is busy actively preparing and doing whatever she can for the baby while she waits for its arrival.

In Acts 16:24-26 Paul and Silas knew something about waiting, and they waited well. They were attacked by a crowd, beaten and thrown in jail. This was not just any jail they were in the inner prison (the dungeon) and their feet were fastened locked in stocks to be sure they wouldn't escape. However, about the midnight hour, God showed up. Now it would have been nice if He had come a little earlier. However, Paul and Silas did not seem to mind—they just decided to start singing and began to worship Him with the other prisoners listening to them praise God while they waited.

How should we wait on the Lord, we first wait in prayer being still before God without saying one word. We cannot and should not offer our petition until we are fully aware of having secured the attention of God. This is accomplished by being obedient to His word inviting and allowing the Holy Spirit to come in and fill our hearts indwelling us so that we are living a life for Him, only then will we have the realization that God has come near.

We also need to wait for His answer with enthusiasm actively serving Him. In doing so just as the expecting mother prepares for the arrival of her baby your waiting serves as a time of preparation for His answer. If God were to answer right away, many of us would not be adequately prepared to handle such a warp-speed solution.

Therefore, He provides a little time during our journey to fasten our seat belts, He sees, then protects us from the turbulence we're in store for up ahead before reaching our destination.

"But they that wait upon the LORD shall renew their strength; they shall mount up with wings as eagles; they shall run, and not be weary, and they shall walk, and not faint," - Isaiah 40:31

Frustrated with God
I'm Not Hanging Around Here Forever!

... "Be still, and know that I am God; I will be exalted among the nations, I will be exalted in the earth." – Psalm 46:10

We all desire good things in life and want the very best things to happen to us in our lives, although most of us have a microwave mentality, we want it all now. However, when it doesn't happen the way we want when we want, we are tempted to question God," When, God, when?" Many of us need to mature in the area of trusting God instead of focusing on the "when" question. There is a propensity for many of us to want to know everything about anything that's going on, some of us even feel we need to know. Knowledge can be detrimental to your Christian walk, particularly if you are not prepared to receive the information you feel you need or are entitled to. Knowing everything about anything can be uncomfortable and may even hurt you. Many people spend a large part of life being impatient, frustrated and disappointed because there were things they didn't know and could not understand. For me, I had to learn to leave things alone and quit feeling that I needed to know everything. God had to teach me and as I finally began to trust the only One, who knows all and learned to accept that some questions may never be answered. I found a lot of my anxiety quickly began to fade, we prove we trust God when we refuse to worry.

Frustration has been defined as the feeling of being upset or annoyed when we think our needs are not being met, or because of our inability to change or accomplish something especially when the problem appears to be insurmountable. Many times your frustration stems from a lack of understanding. It may be regarding a particular situation or a person's behavior or choices. There are times when God will also be the focus of your displeasure and dissatisfaction. Consequently, you may even grow frustrated with God, with His ways, and His dealings with us and this can be a significant stumbling block if you're not careful. We are well aware that when we have a need God already knows and He could easily handle any problem. We begin to feel worried, in a hurry, and out of control concerning whatever it is that is not "going well." All of our concern begs the question and it always seems to boil down to when will He, why won't He, or where is He? Most Christians have found themselves fuming with frustration at God at some point in their lives for something.

Are we wrong for being frustrated with God? We are indeed. Frustration is a product of our humanity our sin nature. Being frustrated with God could be an indication of an absence of trust in God or at the very least a lack of under- standing of who God is. Psalm 18:30 tells us His way is perfect: the word of the LORD is tried: he is a buckler to all those that trust in him. God is perfect, He has flawless intentions, perfect timing, perfect methods, and complete results. In Isaiah 26:3 we read

"Thou wilt keep him in perfect peace, whose mind is stayed on thee: because he trusteth in thee." When you focus your mind on the Lord and trust in Him, you will know peace, not frustration.

When you consider Jonah he knew all too well what is was to be frustrated with God. In Jonah 1:1-3 Jonah heard from God but did not like what he heard. Much like Jonah our frustration with God could be a byproduct of our stubbornness. When our ambitions conflict with God's purposes, we will naturally be frustrated. It is never advisable to fight against God. Saul of Tarsus learned this lesson although he did it the hard way, as Jesus reminded him, "It is hard for you to kick against the goads" Acts 26:14. Frustration can impair our vision while choking our compassion. God would like for us to live by discernment revelation knowledge, in other words, we need to get out of our head. It's difficult to exercise judgment if you're always trying to figure everything out. When you feel frustrated with God, it could be due to a lack of understanding, and not on God's part. A better way to dealing with your frustration with God is to submit to His perfect will, accept His timing as perfect timing, and trust His goodness. "Cast all your cares on him because he cares for you" 1 Peter 5:7.

It's Not My Fault
Well Don't Look at Me I Didn't Do It!

But who can discern their own errors? Forgive my hidden faults -
Psalm 19:12

I am just as certain there is an invisible war going as I am of the many visible battles confronting us daily. While I am very confident of the above fact, I am not so extreme that I see a demon around every corner. I do however believe satan is to blame for much of the evil that continues to manifest itself in the world today. Conversely, it is also believed that all too often Christians use satan as the fall guy, the scapegoat.

During some point in your life, you may have heard the expression: 'The devil made me do it'? Of course you have, that is unless you have had your head stuck in the sand all your life. If we for a moment could be honest with ourselves, most of us have used this phrase in some form on more than one occasion when we have done something rather unscrupulous. It seems to be part of our human nature born out of man's fall from grace to coin yet another familiar phrase to "pass the buck" along to someone else when we commit a shameful act.

More than thirty years have elapsed since a comedian by the name of Flip Wilson kept people in stitches with the portrayal of his fictional television characters. The "Reverend Leroy," was a friendly, yet pompous pastor of the fictitious

"Church of What's Happening Now," and "Geraldine Jones," a sassy African-American woman in a miniskirt. Whenever Geraldine would impulsively spend money—or do anything she shouldn't do—she excused her urge by uttering the unforgettable phrase, "The devil made me do it!" Many laughed at the fictitious character Geraldine and the apparently lame excuse she became known for. In fact, it quickly became a household phrase, it was commonplace to repeat "The devil made me do it," those words quickly swept the country. Of course, we all know that the devil wants us to sin, but everybody knew the truth.

Today we see a very radical theology that seems to be a strange mix between Reverend Leroy and Geraldine. Sadly, it is not difficult to find ministries with leaders who point to the devil and his imps for all the sins that plague us. For example, people are told by some they have a "spirit of divorce," a "spirit of lust," of "neglect," or "procrastination." These types of spirits are regularly blamed for people's sins, and the solution to these iniquities quickly becomes a process of casting out the spirit causing them. Geraldine would be so proud of us.

Often you find the Bible will use the word "spirit" when speaking of a demon. In doing so, a descriptive word or phrase will often be attached. The Bible speaks of "unclean spirit" in Mark 1:23, an "evil spirit" in Acts 19:12-13, a "spirit of infirmity" in Luke 13:11, and a "deaf and mute spirit" in Mark

9:25. The words such as "unclean" and "evil" describe the nature of the spirit itself. But phrases like "spirit of infirmity" and "deaf and mute spirit" represent the particular affliction caused by these spirits. Unfortunately, it is possible for people to launch into theological error by confusing affliction with transgression, and begin the practice of naming a demon after their sin.

We never read in the Bible where it ever speaks of the work of demons in the lives of believers directly relating to immortality. Therefore, when someone says a believer has the "spirit of lust' as though the real culprit is a demon declares something the Bible never teaches. Although it is true, the demonic realm can influence a believer's morality. However, God's Word describes demonic influence in a believer's life not as "possession"—or even "oppression"—but primarily as temptation.

James 1:4 affirms, "Each person is tempted when he is lured and enticed by his own desire." Simply stated we sin because we are sinners. We are plagued by and infected with sin Romans 3:10-23. While demonic oppression and influence are real, the primary problem is our sinful natures. "Now the works of the flesh are evident: sexual immorality, impurity, sensuality, idolatry, sorcery, enmity, strife, jealousy, fits of anger, rivalries, dissensions, divisions, envy, drunkenness, orgies, and things like these" Galatians 5:19-21. Notice, it's the "works of the flesh" on this list, not the works of the devil.

When you are a Christian and sin, the devil is not to blame as the one who made you do it. However, it is possible and in some case very likely that he had a hand in tempting you to do it. He may also have been influential in your decision process to carry out the sin, but he did not make you do it. The choice was always yours, every step of the way.

God is faithful and never allows you to be tempted beyond your ability to withstand the distraction, but when you are tempted, he will also provide a way out so that you can endure it. (1 Corinthians 10:13). When you say "the devil made me do it" you deny the truth found in 1 John 4:4 ..." the one who is in you is greater than the one who is in the world."

Self-deception is the deadliest of all deceit, and of all the deceived people the self-deceived are the least likely to realize they are in a con. When you are deceived by someone, you are being misled against your will. You are contending against an adversary and you become a temporary victim of another's deviousness. Under such conditions, it is possible to be deceived for a short time, but as the victim you are resisting you will most likely escape the snare and escape before much damage is done.

With self-deception, it is quite different. You are your own enemy and working a scam on yourself. You go all in full speed ahead into the deception because want to believe the lie you become completely invested and psychologically conditioned to carrying out the fraud. You do not resist the deceit rather you collaborate with it against yourself. There is no wrestling because you are both the victim and perpetrator and you submit long before the fight begins.

So, how should we respond to temptation and remain free from self-deception? We must know and anchor ourselves in God's Word. When satan tempted Jesus in the wilderness, the devil again tried to mix-up the Word of God, as he did with the woman in the garden. But Jesus not only knew the Scripture, but He also clung to it—and sent the devil packing Matthew 4:1-11. James 4:7 teaches us to use this same proven strategy, "Submit therefore to God. Resist the devil and he will flee from you."

It may seem a bit harsh to tell someone that the problem is them and their choices. But it's no more discordant than a doctor telling a patient to quit smoking or lose weight and that the tobacco company and McDonald's are not to blame for their poor health. To find a cure, you have to start with a correct diagnosis and then move to the proper treatment. The correct diagnosis is sin; the only known treatment is to submit yourself to God and obey His Word. God will enable you to triumph over sin Romans 7:24-25; 1 John 5:3-5. Christians have everything needed to live a life of godliness, here and now therefore if we sin we have no excuse, you cannot blame the devil because you have the indwelling Holy

Spirit to help you overcome all sin. We also cannot blame our circumstances. We only have ourselves to blame. Sadly enough for many until we recognize that the problem resides within us Romans 7:20, we will never arrive at the only solution.

Struggling with Submission
Submit! Are You Kidding Me!

Submit yourselves, then, to God. Resist the devil, and he will flee from you. - James 4:7

This submission thing can be tough; people naturally don't want to submit one to another or any authority figure. True submission is a concept that seems to go against the grain of human nature, and yet we all see the need for it in certain aspects of life. Today we live in the days of pride and rebellion. However, without submission, things quickly fall into chaos as everyone strives to be in charge. Even though it is sometimes mocked as a sign of weakness, submission is one of the strongest pillars of a stable society.

I don't know about you, but I struggle with being submissive. I must admit although the first part of James 4:7 says "Submit yourselves therefore to God "I fall short sometimes when it comes to completely submitting to God. It bothers me when people tell me what to do, how to live, and what I should be doing. I even ignore myself sometimes. When I know, I need to do something, and I don't because I would much rather do something else instead. Personally, I think that is one of the major struggles we all have in our walk with God, the part I cannot for the life of me figure out is why we keep rebelling. Is it that hard?

Well, it must be, all too often we forget that we do not wrestle against flesh and blood, but against the principalities of darkness. - Ephesians 6:12

We read in the book of Ephesians 5:22-25, the wife is to submit to her husband as unto the Lord and the husband is to" love" his wife. The Apostle Peter writes, "Young men, in the same way, be submissive to those who are older. All of you, clothe yourselves with humility toward one another, because, 'God opposes the proud but gives grace to the humble'" 1 Peter 5:5. The theme is one of humility. You are not able to truly submit without first humbling yourself. A person can never submit to God devoid humility. Obedience requires us to humble ourselves to surrender to the authority of another, and we are told that God resists pride—the opposite of humility—and the arrogance that fosters that pride.

As Christians, we are told to submit to one another out of reverence for Christ Ephesians 5:21. This prevents selfish pride and fits well with the command to consider others better than ourselves Philippians 2:3. If our purpose on this earth is to do the will of God, then submitting to someone else becomes an act of trust in God. We naturally look out for our best interests, but, if we trust God to take care of us, then we are free to take care of others.

Therefore, having a humble and submissive heart is a choice we make. That means as a professed born-again believer we make daily choices to submit ourselves to God for the work that the Holy Spirit does in us to" conform us to the image of Christ." God will use circumstances of our lives to bring us the opportunity to submit to Him Romans 8:28-29. The believer then accepts His grace and provision to walk in the Spirit and not in the fashion of the old sin nature. That work is only accomplished by choosing to apply yourself to the Word of God and learning about the provisions that God has made for us in Christ Jesus. From the moment we are born again, we have all the provisions we need in Christ, to become a mature believer. However, we have to make the choice to learn about those necessities through study of the Word and to apply those provisions to our daily walk

We must always humbly present ourselves and submit to authority in a godly fashion. Even if that authority violates God's order, we should submit in a holy manner. When the apostles were arrested for speaking about Jesus, they did not resist. However, when told to stop teaching Jesus, they replied, "We must obey God rather than men!" Acts 5:29. They appealed to a higher authority and continued to preach Jesus openly, even though it led to persecution. In some cases, they saw God bring miraculous deliverance. In others, God allowed martyrdom. In all instances, they rejoiced "because they had been counted worthy of suffering disgrace for the Name" Acts 5:41.

The Bible has many other things to say about submission and is replete with references like those contained in this post. Requiring of us to submit to all authority, this must be our stance as long as it does not contradict the authority of God. You don't follow the directions of an authority figure who asks you to commit a crime. While doing the offense is submitting to the authority, doing what's right is surrendering to God. After all, God is the supreme authority and He alone ultimately overrides all.

Identify Yourself
I Know Who I Am

Yet to all who received him, to those who believed in his name, he gave the right to become children of God. - John 1:12

When you are asked to identify yourself, you probably get out some physical form of ID. There is something you carry on your person at all times that describes you, your physical description and maybe even your relationship with other people, an organization, your state, or country. You might have a driver's license; an employee badge; a passport, a debit or credit card; a library card; a union card; military dog tags or a law enforcement officer's badge. Those are only a few of the many types of IDs we take with us almost everywhere we go. The most common of all of these are a driver's license and a badge to get into and around the buildings where one works.

Identity theft is one of the greatest fears people live with today and this concern has become commonplace in our society, at times even claiming the top spot on the nightly news. The loss of identity can be difficult for anyone. You are faced with routine tasks that have become confusing and situations you don't know how to handle. The need to protect your identity has become increasingly important considering the growing number of social networking and blogging sites available today. Personality profiles and blogging about personal experiences create a public record of you and your personal information. When someone uses your name, personal information, account numbers, and passwords, they can take everything making your life miserable. I can recall having gone looking for a misplaced wallet, and credit card after leaving them behind at a restaurant. The whole time my stomach was churning filled with anxiety about what could happen if it was picked up by the" wrong person."

As important as our identity is regarding finances and possessions, there is an even more vital status based on who and what we are –rather than what we physically own. When a person is asked to describe themselves, a typical male response is to describe himself by what he does or by his career, he's an engineer, or attorney, or auto mechanic, etc. It's among the first things the person talks about when asked to describe themselves. On the other hand, a woman will typically identify herself by her relationships first, those of family, friends, and neighbors; she may first confirm that she is a mother, a wife, a sister. Although not necessarily the majority, these remain typical responses when one is asked to describe themselves.

Unfortunately, these intangible identities can be lost. It happens when children leave home, and that mom is no longer an active mom or when the husband is no longer in the home, and she's not a wife anymore. It happens after a man is laid-off or retires, he's no longer identified as being the attorney, or carpenter, or auto mechanic, or whatever. Over time, these identities become the very purpose of our lives. And their loss can translate into a life no longer having real meaning or purpose for some.

Who are you? This is a question many people struggle to answer. Do you know who you are? I'm not talking about who you are because of your parents, your job, education, or your upbringing, but I mean do you honestly know who you are in Christ?

Too often, people base their identities on what they do from their jobs to their roles in relationships, defining themselves by those pursuits. But by doing so, they significantly limit their lives. The truth is that God desires everyone find their identity in Christ. Look what Peter says to believers who were under intense persecution in 1 Peter 2:9. "But ye are a chosen generation, a royal priesthood, a holy nation, a peculiar people: that ye should shew forth the praises of him who hath called you out of darkness into his marvelous light. " John also has a word in John 1:12 "But as many as received him, to them gave He the power to become the sons of God, even to them that believe on his name." Now let's listen to Paul as he speaks to the converts that comprised the churches in Galatia just over in Galatians 3:26 "For ye are all the children of God by faith in Christ Jesus."

The single most valuable treasure you possess here on earth and yet it remains the least understood is your identity in

Christ. One reason many people have difficulty identifying with Jesus is because they relate to their physical, natural characters and the things they can perceive with their senses more than they do with Him. Until it becomes paramount in our thinking, we will remain stuck in an impossible struggle to make our flesh behave. Now, since it won't behave, others see us as hypocrites trying to act out the role of Christians – failing to do what we say. Knowing who we are in Christ is the catalyst for walking in the power of God and demonstrating that power to the world.

Every person has a worldly or human identity –and each has a spiritual character. 1 John 3:10 tells us that everyone is either a child of God or a child of the devil. As a Christian, it is understood you are a child of God. However, there is so much more to your identity than being a child of the King. It is a vital part of our confidence to know who we are in Christ because this is the area that satan will wage a consistent full on attack against us. In fact, when satan attacked Jesus in the wilderness he challenged His identity but Jesus knows who He is, and whose He is. When satan recognized Jesus had no identity problems satan fled and left Him alone.

Your personal identity how you see yourself is often shaped by your early experiences in life. Maybe your parents said things to you when you were a child that made you doubt your worth. Maybe you were rejected, abandoned or worse. A person's identity directly impacts the way they perceive themselves your identity shapes your core beliefs. Those core beliefs, in turn, drive what you think, say and do.

Jesus was not the first to ever be challenged when it come to identity. Satan first waged an attack on the character of both Adam and Eve in the Garden of Eden. satan attacked the character of both Adam and Eve. Although God created Adam and Eve in His image, they allowed the enemy to deceive them by suggesting that they were not who God created them to be. They believed the lie and, as a result, they took the bait and fell into his trap.

In Colossians 2:10, Paul says we are complete in Christ. We are told in Colossians 2:6 -7; we should walk in Him by living our lives in Him, we should be rooted and built up in Him and strengthened in the faith while overflowing with thankfulness. There is a song we would sing in church, "He is my everything, He is my all" this is exactly how Paul sees Jesus – He is everything!

By relentlessly looking into the mirror of God's Word, we can maintain a real awareness of our identity in Christ. The Word of God will tell us exactly who we are and exactly how we look from God's viewpoint.

It will also reveal to us the areas of our lives that do not line up with God's Word. We should strive to identify with the identity that God has given us.

Our identity is in Christ and if our identity is in anything else then when difficult times come we will be shaken and will find it hard to stand! Our families, job, hobbies or ministry may be excellent and may even be a reflection of our identity, but they can all fail causing us to be lost in the process. Our real identity and security reside in Christ alone.

Although, we possess the power of God inside of us. If the power does not embrace the same mindset that Jesus had about His identity for our own lives, we will never be confident enough to walk in that identity. Renew your mind to who you really are declaring it every day. You are the righteousness of God by your faith, not by works. You are God's beloved child, and He loves you uniquely and unconditionally. No matter what you life throws your way, you are more than a conqueror in His eyes. When you walk in your identity when satan comes to attack our identity in Christ, we must remind him of what is written, and just as he left Jesus alone he will also leave us alone.

Taking the Next Steps
No Thanks! I'm Comfortable Right Here

The LORD makes firm the steps of the one who delights in him; -

Psalm 37:23

Have you ever wondered what it is that seems to be stopping you from taking that next step? What appears to be holding you back from boldly moving forward? Is it the size of the task? Is it the doubt radiating from your friends or even family members? Could it be much simpler, perhaps even the fear of failure? Maybe you are in a zone a comfort zone of sorts a place where you are familiar, maybe one of high security. Well, whatever it is there you are standing on the doorstep of great opportunity brilliantly disguised as an impossible undertaking.

The children of Israel found themselves in this very situation; they were on the edge of entering the Promised Land. In chapter three of the book of Joshua, the Israelites are looking across to Canaan with the River Jordan at flood levels standing in their way Josh. 3:1-17. It seemed as though God had brought them to the east bank of the River Jordan at a most inconvenient time. The more they stood looking, the more impossible the crossing seemed. No boats, no bridges, no nothing.

Faced with very improbable and nearly impossible circumstances, God tells the Israelites to follow the priests into the river. He tells them to take a step of faith. God makes them a promise if they march forward by faith in obedience to Him. He tells them when their feet are firmly in the waters of the river Jordan, He will close off the river, enabling them to cross. Trusting God, they took the next step towards Canaan. Passing through the waters, God proved Himself to be with them and for them in a marvelous way Isiah 43:2.

How about you, have you any rivers you think un-crossable? Well, this story teaches us that there are no God-sized solutions until we get our feet wet, in boldly and believing taking the next step in what we know to be the will of God. Heaven moves to help whenever we step out in faith to obey. Focusing on the Ark, that is to say looking to the Lord is always good Joshua 3:11. Sanctifying yourself, that is prayerfully preparing is always good Joshua 3:5. But while that is all good, looking, praying, and waiting alone is simply not enough. We must be bold and take action by also being willing to get our feet wet Joshua 3:13. If we are going to be obedient to the Will of God and His plan for us, we must take that first step. We must dive into the swelling tide, showing our faith to be large, and our God simply to be.

God has consistently proved His promises to all of us in many unimaginable ways. However, it all begins with our step of faith. What are you waiting for go get your feet wet!

Moving Forward
Hold On, Not So Fast, I'm Not Ready

"Forget the former things; do not dwell on the past. - Isiah 43:18

I remember coming across an old Readers Digest article on the Clemson University athletic program. In the article, someone thought it would be a good idea if rowing were to become a part of the program. However, the then athletic director of the school quickly and quite adamantly took the firm position there would be no rowing team on his watch. He just refused to participate in a sport where the Athletics sat down and operated backward to move forward.

When being obedient to God and following Christ, there is no going, back either. The Apostle Paul when writing to the church at Philippi had a very similar perspective driven by his passion for a never-ending desire for a forever growing and much closer relationship with God. Paul reminds them just as the Olympic runner does not look over his shoulder. The followers of Christ must not be found loitering on their way to Heaven, rather using every ounce of their being they must always be relentless in their pursuit of the finish line and ultimate victory. In Philippians 3:13-14 Paul says, "Brethren, I count not myself to have apprehended but this one thing I do, forgetting those things, which are behind, and reaching forth unto those things, which are before, I press toward the mark for the prize of the high calling of God in Christ Jesus." Just like Paul, we too must always be reaching out, and stretching ourselves forth beyond ourselves toward the upward call of God in Christ Jesus.

The existence of the strenuous persistence and unbridled need of pressing forward into an ever deepening and beautiful relationship with Christ must be paramount in every person desiring to be like Christ. This irrepressible surge forward must first, due to necessity involve a detachment with the past. Looking back, works against going forward. Look what Jesus says in Luke 9:62 "No man, having put his hand to the plow, and looking back, is fit for the kingdom of God." In Philippians 3:13 Paul says to the followers of Christ "Brethren, I count not myself to have apprehended: but this one thing I do, forgetting those things which are behind, and reaching forth unto those things which are before," Paul says the things that are behind us must be forgotten. However, Paul is not advocating we erase them from our memory for most people this is simply not possible, but he is saying forgetting in the sense that we are no longer influenced or affected by them!

For many of us, that is good news because most of us do not want to remember our past in the first place. Now notice Paul himself was a man with a messy past, but when he accepted the fact he had obtained mercy, there was no looking back 1 Tim. 1:13. Besides if God had so magnificently forgotten through Christ as is stated in Hebrew 10:17. Where Paul says "And their sins and iniquities will I remember no more" Paul was not going to remember, nor bring any of that past baggage up either. We also need to forget our past sinful baggage and just run the race that is in front of us. As Paul stated in Hebrew 12: 1 "...let us lay aside every weight, and the sin which doth so easily beset us and let us run with patience the race that is set before us." As followers of Christ, our past before Christ must not be allowed to quarrel with our future in Christ.

Just when you think, you are out of the woods. Poor me, another tough break, I just cannot seem to get ahead... Sound familiar? We also need to forget our past sorrows. The majority if not all of Paul's life and ministry in Christ was full of trials and troubles as described in 2 Corinthians 11:23-28. He wore the battle scars of wrestling with people and fighting with devils, but Paul knew there was no future in just sitting around licking his wounds. As followers of Christ, most realize that the cross always comes before the crown.

Finally, we need to forget our past successes. Paul had a ministry resume I am sure we would all agree that is second to none 2Corinthians 12:11. He planted churches, mentored leaders and written much Scripture, but since his life was not over, there was much more work to be done 2Tim. 2:6-8.

Followers of Christ know and understand that now is not the time to polish our medals, and rest on our laurels.

Followers of Christ know there is no future in the past.

Make today the first day of the rest of your life committed to Him. M ay you begin to totally lean on God. Looking only to Christ as you continue your journey pressing more intensely towards a future that is like a light in the distance that shines brighter and brighter with every step you take towards the mark. Proverbs 4:18.

The Days Ahead
Wait a Minute, I Should Expect What?

"Repent and be baptized, every one of you, in the name of Jesus Christ for the forgiveness of your sins. And you will receive the gift of the Holy Spirit" - Acts 2:38

Have you ever noticed how sad it can be after a holiday or another of the great celebrations of life? We anticipate a type of excitement and expectation of the event. Then, so suddenly, it is over. It would be safe to say most people have experienced the morning after. It may not always be a blue Monday following a great weekend, but after almost any significant turning point in life, there is usually a letdown. After any great success or triumph, after any of the great accomplishments of life, there is usually a reaction, a sobering moment, a falling back of sorts. You can almost feel things slowing down, returning to the routine and the mundane. Nurses have reported the maternity ward of a hospital can be one of the happiest and yet the saddest. We wait nine long months for the birth of the baby; share the excitement of those first few hours or days of its life, but eventually for some there is a period of depression. It is a very dark and gloomy day. The initial rush of excitement is gone; the baby is keeping you up all night. You are tired and discouraged, and you find yourself asking,"Why did I ever get myself into this situation?"

Can you imagine what it might have been like for the Disciples after the Resurrection when they did not actually witness the Resurrection? They had only heard of the empty tomb; a couple of the disciples had even encountered a stranger while they were on the road to Emmaus, but even if it were Jesus, oh well? For them, things seemed to be quickly returning to normal.

Monday after the resurrection was no doubt full of puzzling uncertainty. Like you, the Disciples had to go back to living their lives but how could they merely move on with the business of living. Again, like you, they did so with a sometimes-faltering faith. In fact, one could reason that is why Jesus returned several times, maybe to prove to them He was alive, and they had a truth to share. He appeared, and then left them to wonder and try to sort it out. The Monday after the resurrection may have been a bit standard as far as normal goes. Somehow, the Disciples had to go on about their normal daily activities. Just like you.

Even if you could, like Thomas, reach in and touch the wounds in his body. Even if you had solid, certifiable evidence that the resurrection was real, and it is. You would still have bills to pay, meals to plan, along with all the other concerns of this life. Much like it was for His first Disciples.

In many ways, I am sure; most Christians today face the same challenge: how do you live in the glory of the Resurrection? On the other hand, as Paul asked, how do you "know the power of His resurrection?" The simplest response would be through faith, each day, you cling to the fact of His life. He is not just a memory or a "Spirit that is still with us." Paul's constant refrain is that Christ is not only alive but that He is alive in you.

If it is your desire to be a true Disciple of Jesus, we must begin thinking and demonstrate our care and concern about the fate of ALL of God's children throughout this entire world. Not only that of our families, neighbors, friends, or people we choose to like. Much like the first Disciples, we are challenged to build a community of faith that crosses every border and hurdles every barrier separating people one from the other.

How are we to begin?

Much like Jesus did when he appeared to His Disciples for the third time in John 21:12-13 -" Jesus said to them, "Come and have breakfast. "Jesus came, took the bread and gave it to them, and did the same with the fish." His interaction was a very simple yet powerful act of care, concern, and love. Here is the risen Christ, the Lord of Lords and King of Kings, serving and enjoying a casual breakfast by the sea conversing with His friends. Thank God, for all the simple things in life, many of which are free. When you consider your morning after you may discover it is enough to offer a gift to a friend. Cook a meal for somebody; send an email, text, or call someone you have not spoken with or seen for a while or maybe smile at a stranger.

For many Resurrection, Sunday is the first day of the rest of your life. For others, it serves as a very real reminder. He did not just rise from the dead one Sunday; he is alive forever, this is the message of the Gospel. Resurrection Sunday is not just another moment in time or merely a one-day event in History. He lives in every believer. Eternal life will not begin at some point in the future. The Monday after and all the days following Easter and throughout all eternity, we are all to be a living witness to the reality of the living God.

The question is how are you going to live with that reality?

Learning to Trust God
Trust is Something You Earn Not Learn

Those who know your name trust in you, for you, Lord, have never forsaken those who seek you. - Psalm 9:10

For years, I have had the habit of trusting no one other than myself which made my life very chaotic, to say the least. I developed this unfortunate habit through many years of trusting people, getting hurt and finding out I couldn't trust them. My distrust led me to believe what I'd always been told, if you want something done right, you've got to do it yourself. If you never ask anybody for anything or open your heart to them, they can't hurt you and you won't owe them anything. But this mindset only kept me from trusting God. It was a bad habit I had to break. It somewhat saddens me when I think of how mush time I wasted during those early years of living this way. I was a Christian and would attend church. Unfortunately, I spent a lot of time doing stupid things, making bad decisions, and being upset over things I couldn't control. I experienced feelings of guilt and condemnation most of the time, had no peace and just didn't enjoy life very much at all.

Suddenly I begin going through a very radically life transformation. I listened and learned to change my entire way of thinking and have since made it a habit of really trusting God for everything, and now I am living a joyful, peaceful life worth living. God wants us to put Him first in our lives. He wants us to put ALL of our confidence and trust in Him, ALL the time, in EVERYTHING.

Most people would not readily have confidence in someone they didn't know. When someone says to you, "Trust me," you will have one of two reactions. Either you say, "Yes, I'll have faith in you," or you say, "No, why should I, I don't even know you." In God's case, trusting Him naturally follows when we understand why we should. Understanding the "why" is the biggest key to learning and establishing trust in God. Learning to trust God will only be realized when you acknowledge His complete character and His track record of perfection.

King Solomon wrote in the book of Proverbs 3:5, 6 "Trust in the Lord with all your heart and lean not on your own understanding; in all your ways submit to him, and he will make your paths straight." When you accept Jesus Christ as your Savior, the Spirit of God comes to live inside you. Having God on the inside is one of the greatest blessings of your salvation: Knowing you will never have to go through someone else to get to God. He lives in your heart, as you begin to trust Him, you will learn to hear His voice.

The best way to receive the voice of God when you hear it, and understand how to live the life He wants for is to consistently follow Him, His Word, says. God's Word gives us wisdom. As we walk with Him, by searching the Bible for His words, the Apostle Paul speaks to our heart in Romans 12:2, encouraging you "Do not conform to the pattern of this world but be transformed by the renewing of your mind. Then you will be able to test and approve what God's will is-his good, pleasing and perfect will". So we should no longer merely think the way the world thinks, when we learn to follow after and walk with God we can think the way God thinks! I have discovered that some of the greatest manifestations in the Bible have come as a result of complete reliance and confidence in God. I have also learned that many times people will believe God, and believe in God, but they don't trust Him. I think we often confuse the two. When we trust God, we rely on and depend on Him to work out all of your situations in life.

When you trust God, it's like following directions using your phone, or GPS mapping device to reach a particular destination. When you need to travel to a location you've never been before, and someone who has provides you with directions, you don't question them. You merely follow the instructions you are given trusting the person knows how to get you to your desired destination. The possibility for you to get lost a time or two remains, however, it may be because you misunderstood part of the directions, or perhaps you missed a turn, or even tried to take a shortcut. However, you can always call that person to clarify the directions getting you back on track on your journey. In like fashion, you must call on God for directions in life. He gives us directions through the Holy Spirit and His Word. When you miss that turn in life, that road sign when you take the wrong road at the fork or even make a mistake by setting the cruise control and begin to drift off track. God will direct you, making sure you get back on the right road at the right time.

To develop complete trust in the Lord, it helps to read the Bible regularly, it is not enough to know about God, or to know of God, we must cultivate our relationship with Him to know Hom intimately every day. The way you develop your confidence in others is by spending time with them, we will learn to trust God the same way. When we spend time with Him, by meditating on His Word in the Bible and reading His Words daily. Also, spending time with God regularly in prayer is another way to develop a consciousness of His presence, which helps us develop our trust in Him.

On the other hand, when we decide to trust our feelings, education, perceptions, or our way of doing things, we say to God, "I don't trust your way." Not trusting God is nothing more than pride. However, when you make the decision to trust God and place your faith in Him at all costs by your free will when you make the Word of God the final and only authority in your life no matter what it may look like to the world. You begin to demonstrate humility through your trust in His directions, and you will experience His best in every situation of your life.

You may struggle to believe that the Lord will provide for your daily needs. Perhaps you're facing an overwhelmingly difficult time in your life—a time that drains you in every way while exhausting ALL your resources you've reached your capacity in every way. Or perhaps you wonder if He will ever fulfill your heart's desire in a particular area. Trusting the Lord means looking beyond what you can see, so you can look in the direction of what God sees. David won the victory over Goliath—an experienced, intimidating warrior—not because he was smarter, or stronger than his opponent but because the young shepherd was able to see the conflict from God's perspective. Where will you place your trust?

A Wise Decision
That Remains to Be Seen

"...I have set before you life and death, blessings and curses. Now choose life, so that you and your children may live... "-
Deuteronomy 30:19

Have you ever considered the decisions you make each day? If you were just to stop and take a moment to think about it, you might determine the number to be in the hundreds. From the time we wake up in the morning, we begin making decisions. We first decide if we are going to get out of bed, which side of the bed, will you make it now or brush your teeth first, perhaps you'll wash your face. What will you eat for breakfast, will you cook, eat a bowl of cold cereal, or go to a restaurant, will you even eat breakfast at all, and on and on. While it may seem like these type of choices along with many of our daily choices are not that significant, it's important to understand that all your choices do matter.

Our lives are comprised of a series of decisions. While we would like to believe more often than not that our misfortunes are the fault of others, but to blame someone else, God, or even the devil is not the answer to our own wrong choices. But keep in mind that God can take our questionable or even our bad decisions and use them to help us fulfill His will. You should not feel guilty about bad decisions. We have all made them, and chances are we will all make more in this life. However, you must be willing to take responsibility for your wrong choices and make a firm decision to change the way you behave. When you do, it will become evident that your right choices play an intricate role in assisting to reverse the wrong decisions you've made in the past. Unfortunately, many people take on the role of the victim and blame others for their mistakes in life, and they stop making progress.

When God says in Deuteronomy 30:19 to "choose life," He is showing us what wisdom looks like – its life is giving. When you follow wisdom, you will live much deeper than your superficial "wants, thoughts, or emotions" real wisdom will always choose to act now with a view to later gratification and the understanding knowledge of lasting satisfaction. Foolishness acts without common sense acting on the belief that the choices made in the moment will bring about an immediate satisfaction with lasting gratification.

Many times in my life the Lord had to place me back on the right road when I tried to fulfill my will instead of His will. While it is true, God has made us free moral agents, in other words, we have free will to choose, and He will never violate our right to choose. In other words, He will tell us what to do, and allow us to determine whether we will do it.

The wisdom we need to manage our lives comes from God's Word, and whatever contradicts His Word will always lead us down the wrong road. We do not have to look hard to find information that opposes Him and His very existence. There is opposition all around just look at your local media outlet, we witness it on television, we hear it being broadcast over the airwaves on the radio, we even read it in our books and magazines. Those who regularly produce misinformation only seek to affirm the social norms and satisfy the values of our self-serving society.

But how do you get the godly wisdom to make the right decisions when you don't know everything in the Bible? What if you need to make a decision that is not in the Bible, such as how to choose the best car? James 1:5, says, "If any of you lacks wisdom, you should ask God, who gives generously to all without finding fault, and it will be given to you."

If you need wisdom, ask for it, and God will impart His insight into you. Asking God for wisdom is but one of the many ways of acknowledging Him in all your ways. When you choose the world's way of doing things over God's way, you shouldn't be surprised when your plans don't work out the way you envisioned.

In John 14:6 Jesus says ..." I am the way and the truth and the life."

Choose wisely, choose Life, choose Jesus!

Discover Your Life
Uh, Hello It Wasn't Lost

For whoever wants to save their life will lose it, but whoever loses their life for me will save it. - Luke 9:24

Your life is intended to be a dazzling expression of all that God is. Today, people are searching like never before for answers to the age-old question, "what is the meaning of life?" They want to know about, life, death, and all that happens in between, people are also curious and want to know what happens beyond this life. Most people are aware when they become engaged in conversations about our existence, more often than not personal opinions regarding life and death are formed. Through those opinions "logical" conclusions are reached, these findings, of course, are based on nothing more than our individual finite intellect.

Most people begin their day striving to conduct their life according to the conscious and subconscious guidelines that have already been laid out for them by parents, family, and society. You believe you are for the most part honest, a good person, someone thought of as responsible, a person considered to be reliable by some, and reasonable by most. Yet there are some who would admit, there is a voice deep down on the inside saying," I can't do this anymore, I feel like I'm suffocating." We can often find ourselves in places where we feel trapped, stuck, stagnant if you will, in the routine of this thing called life. In an ongoing effort to find life, we find ourselves chasing memories in time. We often reminisce of happy moments in our life as though chasing these moments, will reveal our value, our reason for being, our purpose in life.

Many times as Christians we don't realize the importance of operating according to the guidelines established by God in all areas of our lives. Far too often and before we know it, we substitute religion for a real relationship with Jesus. We often think we are cultivating a relationship with Him when we are doing nothing more than "Christian-like things," and living as if those things are enough. Although, you can certainly appreciate the facts of Jesus' death and resurrection. However, until you have made Him your Lord, those facts do you no good (John 3:16–18; Acts 10:43; Romans 10:9). There is a difference between intellectual assent and a relationship where you know Jesus.

Knowing Jesus means you have accepted His sacrifice on your behalf (2 Corinthians 5:21). You invite Him in to be Lord of your life (John 1:12; Acts 2:21). You identify with Him in His death and recognize your former self to have died with Him (Colossians 3:3; Romans 6:2, 5; Galatians 6:14; 2:20). You accept His forgiveness and cleansing from sin. You seek to know Him in a very intimate fellowship through His Holy Spirit (John 17:3; Philippians 3:10; 1 John 2:27). At the end of the day, you want to be exactly like Him.

Today millions of people have an idea of Jesus, that is to say, they are familiar with a few things about Him. Many have even memorized what they believe to be relevant Bible verses, some even attend church with some form of regularity. Unfortunately, they have yet to allow the facts of Jesus to become their personal reality. They maintain words in their heads never allowing the words to become their truth a truth that would enter into their hearts. Jesus explains the problem in Matthew 15:8-9 when he says "These people honor me with their lips, but their hearts are far from me. They worship me in vain; their teachings are merely human rules.."

While many profess to serve God, they rely on self and their own efforts to follow Him, they trust only themselves to form a right character, and it is in their own good works that their hope lies to secure salvation. For these people their hearts are not moved by the love they have of Christ, but because they seek to perform the duties they believe God requires of them to gain heaven. For the one that has invited Christ into their heart religion is worthless. When Christ dwells in the heart, the soul will be so filled with His love, with the joy of fellowship with Him, that it will cleave to Him; and in the contemplation of Him, one's self will be forgotten.

In Matthew 7:22 Jesus says "Not everyone who says to me, 'Lord, Lord,' will enter the kingdom of heaven, but only the one who does the will of my Father, who is in heaven. Many will say to me on that day. 'Lord, Lord, did we not prophesy in your name, and your name drive out demons and in your name perform many miracles?' Then I will tell them plainly, 'I never knew you. Away from me, you evildoers!" There were those that during the time of Jesus, saw Him as nothing more than an excellent Teacher of high moral standards. They believed they were friends of His because they knew the Law he spoke of. They would listen to His teaching, and some would even follow Him As it is today there were those who often celebrated the miracles, and liked most of what He said. But for Jesus, they would be nothing more than "evildoers" that he has never known.

God has made a very personal promise to you, He says "Ye shall seek Me, and find Me when ye shall search for Me with all your heart." Jeremiah 29:13. In giving ourselves to God, we must give up all that would separate us from Him. The very nature of God is so vast and complex that it is impossible for the human mind to fully know Him. Therefore, your life is an endless journey of seeking Him, learning about Him, how to Love Him, and learning how to enjoy His fellowship. It is with your whole heart, that you must yield to God, this is the only way for you to be restored to His likeness as it was intended from the beginning. In Matthew 22:37 Jesus explains the greatest commandment "'Love the Lord your God with all your heart and with all your soul and with all your mind." It is because of our sinful nature that we are alienated from God.

God wants to show you His specific will for your life, He wants to share His plan for your life with you, He wants you to know and understand His purpose for your life, allow Him to lead you to it (Psalm 32:8). You will not find the answer anywhere else, and you certainly will not find it on your own. You may have already discovered small pieces of His plan for your life; however, it is a guarantee you will not be completely satisfied until you know, with certainty, what He has called you to do.

If you believe, you have already discovered God's will for your life. Take care to yield entirely to His guidance always presenting yourself to Him as a living sacrifice (Romans 12:1).

Balancing Life
Not a Problem I'm Great at Multi-Tasking

"But seek ye first the kingdom of God, and his righteousness; and all these things shall be added unto you." - Matthew 6:33

Feeling out of sorts lately, unbalanced, as if life is beating you down, causing you to feel bruised, and abused, a little on edge. There are times in life when things seem to get so bad that running away appears to be your best and only option. That is why each day people quit their jobs, leave their homes, families, drop out of school; some may even drop out of society altogether. They have run out of steam, and so they run and run and run only to find themselves traveling in circles in a wilderness situation much like the children of Israel.

You very well may at times find yourself envious of the birds that fly carefree through the skies and wish that you too could migrate to another place, much warmer, sunnier, and friendlier. In the book of Psalms 55:6-8, we notice the King, David envying the birds above his head. His current situation is so painful that he wishes he had the wings of a dove to fly away and find peace. Finding a balance in life does not necessarily mean completely clearing your calendar, but it does require scrutiny of your activities. Have you ever tried examining each activity or appointment from God's point of view. Is the action necessary in your life?

Does your participation in it glorify God's name? Does it distract you from following God's will?

If your desire is to develop balance in your life, you may want to start by asking the question who or what is in control of my life. Do the schedule, agendas, sporting events, aerobics, dance lessons, kids, spouse, work or carpools dominate your time and energy? Do emails, social media, text messages, and cell phones distract you from the real priorities of life? Is the current busy pace of your life leaving you overwhelmed and weary?

If personal desires, appointments, and activities are your driving force, then it is possible that you are allowing selfish thoughts to dominate your life. If you are not careful, your life can become nothing more than a whirlwind of endless activities that leave behind nothing of eternal value. If, on the other hand, Jesus Christ is seated on the throne of your heart. If He, in fact, is your sole motivation, you will discover balance is not only possible but simple. A balanced life is an endless journey of faith and unwavering trust in Him learning to maximize the moment while glorifying the Lord's name every minute.

In the 22nd chapter of the book of Genesis God makes a request of Abraham to place his son on the altar, his son the most precious gift God could have given him. Abraham's heart surely pounded as he climbed to the top of Mount

Moriah with his son Isaac. He had offered many sacrifices, but this one was different. God asked Abraham to trust Him. Before Abraham could complete God's request, God intervened no doubt He was satisfied with Abraham completely surrendering to His will and provided a ram to take Isaac's place.

Are you willing to trust God completely, without question, or reason, even with that which is most precious to you? God wants more than your spare time and juggled schedules. He wants to be Lord of everything, family, meals, laundry, homework, sports activities, leisure time and above all you. No matter how painful the situation you are facing, you can trust God. Stop wasting time, energy, and opportunities trying to bargain with God because you continue doing things your way.

We see King David after being betrayed, by someone who pretended to be on his side, this person was exposed proven to be an enemy and now the leader of the opposition. So, we see David in Psalm 55. He moves from praying to complaining, to finally calling on God, Notice what David did in Psalm 55:22 to handle the situation the solution to his troubles were not found by him running away from his problem but running to the Lord with the problem. It was for David an escape of sorts, but it was an escape toward the presence of God where nourishing grace is found. David realized there was an alternative to running from or through troubles in life. The alternative is being and remaining in the presence of God under His sustaining grace and His strength He enables us to stand up to life. The Lord did not promise to save us from the burdens of life, but to sustain us in them.

It is His presence in and through us by way of worship, prayer, and praise. Enabling us to exchange the wings of a dove as the Psalmist says in Psalm 55:6 for the wings of an eagle as we see in Isaiah 40:31. Doves tend to fly out front carefully getting ahead of the storm, but eagles soar well above the storm gliding along.

God asks that we love Him, trust Him, and obey Him. He is our ALL the Lord of our past, present, and our future. When we accept God as being in control of our lives, we quickly realize nothing ever surprises Him we can trust Him with any and everything. However, God's plan will not happen on your schedule. Do not allow trivial matters to squeeze out what matters in your life. Seek God above career, relationships, money, and even ministry. Jesus is speaking in Matthew 6:33 says "But seek ye first the kingdom of God and his righteousness, and all these things shall be added unto you."

Remember it is your heart attitude that holds the foundation of balance for your life, Matthew 6:21 tells us "For where your treasure is, there will your heart be also." Your response to God and His direction is crucial. Your obedience should be

made an offering to the Lord. Choose to relinquish your"
rights" lovingly and just obey Him. As your life honors and
serves God, He will magnify you knowing you will bring the
focus and glory to Him. Remain focused on the Lord in the
midst of ALL THINGS and he will direct your path.

Consider Your Focus
I Have, This Whole Thing Remains Blurry

If anyone, then, knows the good they ought to do and doesn't do it, it is sin for them. - James 4:17

Two Christians stood talking with one another when one of them said, "Today has been a great day, I have not done anything to be ashamed." The other replied, "I have not had such a good day I have not accomplished anything today to be proud of." In this conversation, we have two very different perspectives on life and how to measure success. One is defined negatively, and one is defined positively.

The first person measures success by defining how much they have not done anything considered to be prohibited or reprehensible. This person believes if they could make it through the day without committing an inexcusable act meaning they did not rob, cheat, lie, kill, or steal then they have succeeded as good for the day. The second person has a very different idea of success. This person believes there is more to being a Christian than measuring the success of your day by the things you do or do not do. Good is never solely determined by what you did or did not do.

James seems to somewhat agree with the second of the two people in James 4:17 where he reminds the Jewish Christians "If anyone, then, knows the good they ought to do and doesn't do it, it is sin for them." James, who is also called James the

Just, and believed to be the half-brother of Jesus, reminds the reader that sin is not just wrongdoing but failure to do right. Sin is not only the act of committing an evil deed, but it is also the omission of performing a good deed. Many only view sin as the presence of evil or the carrying out of an evil or unjust act yet we see James explain that sin is also the absence of good. Are even aware that you disappoint God when you fail to do what you know you should do equally as much as when you do the things you know you should not do but find yourself doing them anyway. Some of the greatest struggles a Christian will ever have is not what they should not do, but those things they fail to do when they know they should do and don't.

The apostle Paul beginning in chapter 4 of his Ephesian letter that is believed written to the church at Ephesus reminds those non-Jewish followers of Christ who long for the Christ-like maturity that they must do more than simply not doing certain things. Paul not only tells them what things they must not do including putting off falsehood, but that is also to say, they must stop lying. He also tells them what they must do in that they must speak the truth. Paul tells them they must not steal, rather they must work with their hands and they must get rid of all bitterness, rage and anger, brawling and slander, along with every form of malice. Replacing these things with compassion and love one to another.

I recall reading where the great British Baptist preacher Charles Spurgeon, was once in the company of a man who spoke very highly of his own virtues making them the primary topic of conversation. Unfortunately, all his supposedly good attributes focused on all the wrong things he had not done. Disappointed and somewhat disgusted with what he perceived as self-righteousness posturing Spurgeon accused the man of being full of negatives. "You do not drink, you do not gamble, you do not swear." Spurgeon went on saying "what in the name of goodness do you do?" Unfortunately, this man like so many today was missing the mark working from only one side of the road. While it is good not to participate in some things, it simply is not good enough. Jesus did not come only to prevent you from being bad, he came so that we would be made positively good brand new. He says "Therefore if any man be in Christ, he is a new creature: old things are passed away; behold, all things become new."

Consider this - By focusing on doing nothing bad, you are doing more harm to the Kingdom of God than those who practice works of iniquity and knowingly endanger the souls of the lost.

You Can Say No
Gee Thanks After All It Is My Life

"For the grace of God has appeared that offers salvation to all people. It teaches us to say "No" to ungodliness and worldly passions and to live self-controlled, upright and godly lives in this present age,"

Titus 2:11-12

During a noon lunch, break on a busy construction site the workers all stop to have a bite to eat. As one of the workers unpacked his lunch he became so disgusted, he stopped held a sandwich in his hand. Looking at the sandwich he says "unbelievable, peanut butter, and jelly again, utterly ridiculous this is the eighth straight day." A co-worker then responded, "Maybe, you should be nice when you ask your wife to make you something different for lunch." "No, that's not it, you don't understand," the man replied, "I live alone; I prepare and pack my own lunch." Although this is a funny little story, I am afraid the joke is on us. Many of us often complain about our schedule being too full, which is probably true, but the most disturbing truth is we packed much of it ourselves. Most people find it hard to say no when asked to get involved with real opportunities, and good causes. Most of us are simply unable to find the common ground, the balance between work, rest, and play.

Nevertheless, why, is it that hard to distinguish between what God tells us to do, and what others and even we believe we should be doing? As parents, employees, employers, members of society, and of course as servants of God, we want to be good stewards, so we think we should be doing it all in the name of God. You are constantly trying to divide yourself equally, among all these things throughout your day, always running until you just run out of fuel. Ignoring all the warning lights on the instrument panel of your brain. You also ignore the still small voice of reason. The voice is telling you your fuel level is low, insisting you can squeeze another mile or so out before refueling. Many times you even unintentionally ignore God telling you that you are running low on the main components of your life. Never realizing if you continue without checking it out you will run until you have absolutely nothing left, damaging that part of your life or worse yet your entire engine. Your busyness can, will and in many cases has already led to emptiness. Families are fractured or broken, your relationships with friends and neighbors are shallow if at all, and your health is constantly overheating causing multiple issues, above all your walk with God has become lifeless and ineffective. The fact is a car without the proper balance of fuel, maintenance, and care is un-drivable, just as a life without fuel, maintenance, and care becomes unlivable.

God created you and always knows all your needs, He knows the who, what, where, when, and why, of your needs and how you need whatever it is that you need so that everything you need can be used for His purpose. Just as you care for your vehicle by following the manufacturers use specifications and maintenance plan; you must do the same for your life. Let's suppose a friend is moving and needs your help. They want you to help move a few items in your car, so you pack your little Honda to the brim even tying furniture on the top, you begin driving, you smell smoke and your little car stops and stalls. This is where learning how to and saying "NO" begins. Society seemingly demands more without providing the means, but it is you who must slow down the snowball effect of doing more things with less, less time, less capacity, and less energy. However, saying yes to saying no is not easy for most people. When you consider life is short, eternity long, and the needs are great all around you. Although those things may all be true, it is also true that you can end up doing many good things that are not wrong at all. However, they are just not right for you, and it would be wrong to give time to them. Remember, if satan cannot make you bad, he will keep you busy. You absolutely must learn to say "NO."

Jesus has no problem saying no. Jesus did not meet every need all the time (Mark 1:35-39). People were going around sick and unhealed while He moved about from one town to another preaching the good news. Jesus spent thirty years in training for the work before Him, yet He only spent three actually performing the work for which He trained. Jesus never tried to do it all. However, He did finish the work His Father gave Him to do (John 17:4).

You must learn to say "NO" redeeming the time is not doing more. Redeeming the time is all about learning what the will of God is for your life, and doing it (Eph. 5:15-17). Redeeming the time is what we do, not how much we do. Doing one more thing is not the same as living wisely. You must learn to say "NO" because we all have a different calling on our lives with varying gifts and talents (1 Cor. 12:12-31; 1 Pet. 4:10-11). You are a unique a perfectly formed jigsaw piece within God's eternal plan. Your individual role is very distinct, not necessarily universal. Remember God has not called you to do it all; He has called you to do specific things that only you can do alongside others who are doing unique things so that it all fits together.

A New Life to Share
I Never Share, Please Stay in Your Lane

" ...your real life is hidden with Christ in God. And when Christ, who is your life, is revealed to the whole world, you will share in all his glory".
Colossians 3:1-4

A Pakistani schoolgirl underwent reconstructive surgery in Britain after being shot in the head at point-blank range by the Taliban for advocating girls' education. Surgeons had to attach a titanium plate to bridge a gap in her shattered skull. The young girl said she felt much better and was focused on her mission of helping others." Today I can speak, and I am getting better day by day," she said in a message recorded before the surgery. Speaking clearly but with a slight stiffness in her upper lip. The student thanked her many supporters around the world: "All of those who have prayed for me and because of these prayers God has given me a new life."

A New Life, He has given all of us the opportunity to have an NEW LIFE have you shared that information with anyone lately? It might be at home or running errands. I cannot say that my life is on a platform, nor do I have a story to share as did the young girl but how we can share Jesus where we are. The small examples in our lives can often have a butterfly effect. What may be small and insignificant to us can be transformed into the greatest encouragement and perhaps even life altering word for someone else. Many Christians do not share Jesus because they are intimidated by the very idea of sharing their faith with anyone. It is not the intent of Jesus for the Great Commission to be an impossible burden. God wants you to be witnesses of Jesus Christ through the natural outcome of your life as you live for him. People make it complicated. Many think they must complete some difficult course on evangelism and apologetic before they can begin sharing Jesus. However, God has designed a natural evangelism program. He made it simple for you all that is left to do is to just get started.

"However, I consider my life worth nothing to me; my only aim is to finish the race and complete the task the Lord Jesus has given me—the task of testifying to the good news of God's grace."- Acts 20:24

Notice the verse does not say the most important thing in life is to go to college, have a great career, get married, start a family, fund your retirement, travel a lot, become famous, or pay off the house. Although these things are undoubtedly important, however, they are not the most important. It says the most important thing in life is to fulfill your mission. God has placed you on earth in the exact position for a purpose. Jesus sacrificed by dying on the cross for you so that you would be able to live out your purpose. God has assigned you a task only you are able to accomplish. Part of your mission is to tell others the Good News of His grace. The way for you to show your gratitude for the many mercies and the abundant grace of God is by making your life count. To live a life of extravagant generosity, and sharing the Good News with as many people as you can.

Worship My Way
No Thank You I'm Good, You Do You

"The way of fools seems right to them..." Proverbs 12:15

There is an erroneous idea continuing to grow silently today in our current society. There are those who believe the primary reason for attending church worship is to "get something from the service," rather than going to GIVE YOUR WORSHIP to God. Going to receive rather than give what a selfish motive on our part all about me. Much like the song made famous by Frank Sinatra "My Way". It is difficult for people to be satisfied attending a worship service if their focus is not on the purpose of attending worship, to Praise and Worship God. We have veered off course as a civilization, as a society, for two reasons. We have refused to look to a transcendent, supreme God for moral absolutes; we have depended instead on our depraved determination of right and wrong.

When a man does not properly worship God, he will often make a god of or for himself then offer his god a piece of the pie so to speak. People even want to "do their own thing" in the worship service of the church. All through the ages, man has sought to make gods that would aid and encourage him in his chosen lifestyle. Usually, these man-made gods whom a man would shower with gifts, offerings and sacrifices deified a man's pet vices. When man enjoyed drinking, he made himself a god for the occasion Bacchus, who smiled on wine and revelry. He wanted to make war on his enemies, so he made himself a god named Mars, who promised victory in battle. For many it seems as though the description of Worship spoken of in the Bible is of no consequence to most so long as they are happy and feel good. We must concern ourselves with what God says about how He is to be worshiped instead of what we might want to offer Him in worship.

Our country continues to create and develop people who are the very best in all of the entertainment and sporting industries the world over. Today we boast more forms of amusement than has ever been known to man, yet still we want more. We are living in an age where everything is designed to appeal to our emotions and entertain us. We have all but forgotten the purpose of the worship service which is to glorify and honor God. There is no place for our own personal entertainment in worship. In fact, God said this same thing to the nation of Israel thousands of years ago. "My people have committed two sins: They have forsaken me, the spring of living water, and have dug their own cisterns, broken cisterns that cannot hold water.." (Jeremiah 2:13)

Although there is nothing wrong with listening to a lovely choir sing. When you come to church with a focus on the music, and desire to have the choir sing for you and concerts to entertain you, you unfortunately are not worshiping God. You have instead become the spectator who is being entertained. Worship is not a spectator event. We dare not become spectators because when you worship, there is an audience of one, God.

Please do not do as most have done and reverse the roles. You certainly can not expect divine will to conform to what seems right in your eyes. In the book of Proverbs 12:15 it says, "The way of the fool is right in his own eyes." The emphasis in this generation is becoming more and more about how the worship service can be more entertaining so the church service is more inviting to please the people and not to please Him.

Worship of God is nothing less than holy and sacred. To distort and reduce it to an entertainment venue in an attempt to "get something out of the service" only to please and gratify ourselves is on par with blasphemy. The purity of true worship must not be sacrificed on the altars of entertainment-oriented quartets, choirs, famous preachers, teachers, leaders, other entertainment groups. We are as to do as Hebrews 13:15" offer the sacrifice of praise to God, the fruit of our lips, giving thanks to His name." While in worship, we must always be the participants, and never the observers.

Galatians 1:10 the question is asked," Do I seek to please men? For if I still pleased men, I would not be a servant of Christ." If you desire your worship to be more meaningful and spiritually uplifting, it must always be God-centered. If you want your worship to be acceptable to God, then your worship must never be man-centered. When you seek an emotional high from worship and you, do not receive it, you will become disappointed in everything that has to do with worship even God. The desire to have an experience or an encounter along the lines of mysticism also gives little regard to what God says in the Bible.

Your worship of God requires commitment on your part. Many would rather worship Christ as a babe in a manger than Christ as their crucified savior. They're praising Christ as a baby in a manger requires no commitment on their part. They feel they can put Him in a box and live the rest of the year as they please. Worshiping Christ as your crucified savior requires a life long commitment, a complete change and relinquishing of your life. A total surrender with a committed willingness to do all that He would have you to do. Jesus says in Matthew 10:37," He who loves father or mother more than Me is not worthy of Me. And he who loves son or daughter more than Me is not worthy of Me."

God through Jesus must be first in our lives, and this requires one hundred percent of you, your full commitment.

Let Go
Of What? I'm Not Holding Anything

"Cast your cares on the Lord and he will sustain you;"
Psalm 55:22

The primary cause of stress in your life is much worry. You worry because you become concerned that you may not have what you need when you need it. But anytime you rely on yourself or others to meet those needs outside of God, you will become frustrated and heading into a season of disappointed because nobody can meet all your needs. There is a very familiar phrase "Let go and let God" it seems so straightforward and, of course, it is easier said than done. Unfortunately, we aren't always clear about what it is we're supposed to let go of. Then there are other times we grip so tightly to assumptions about the way our life "should" be. We believe things should be so much easier or living life shouldn't be so hard.

Some people find security in their job, and when they lose their job, they also lose their peace of mind. Others put their confidence in their spouse or their marriage. Then when their spouse is no longer available, or they go through a divorce, they begin to ask, "Who am I? What is my identity?" Your identity is everything it is who you are your possessions, your life, your accomplishments, your experiences, your attitudes, your past, your hopes, and dreams, etc. All of these are the framework for who you are. It has taken or will take most of us a lifetime just to fit into this world. Even if you have already achieved much, marked your territory and let the world know what you believe in. It is your identity, your ego and persona, how you see yourself and how others perceive you is ultimately all that you keep. Our identity gives us purpose and direction in life. But it is also your identity that may prevent God from using you. For so many, there is a very condescending me first attitude...even before God.

Many put their security in money, even with the knowledge of there being a lot of ways to lose money. This information may just be common sense, but we should all refrain from placing our security in anything that can be taken away from us. You can lose your job, your health, your reputation, your spouse, and your mind. But you cannot lose your relationship with Christ. When you put your security in His promises, you can trust God to meet all your needs.

Too often we fight even rebel against what we're being asked to do. We want to live free from all worry, yet when the requirements for such a life are provided in the form of absolute surrender we struggle. This is not an option it is a requirement Jesus explained in Matthew 16:24 – 26 while speaking to His disciples, He says "...Whoever wants to be my disciple must deny themselves and take up their cross and follow me. For whoever wants to save their life will lose it, but whoever loses their life for me will find it".

Sometimes you need to give up the preconceived notions of how your or life around you is supposed to work. After all "What good will it be for someone to gain the whole world, yet forfeit their soul?"

Far more often than not there is a difference between your desire to give something up and the actual need to release it. You may hold tight to something or the idea of a thing you believe to be good. This could even be something very positive like a change in the behavior of a wayward child, or you may not want to give up praying for the improved health of a loved one. Although it is never wrong to desire good things, there are times when we must let go of what we think is best.

If you really want to find God, you must let go of your identity, your feelings, your relationships, your possessions, your principals, and even your concept of who God is. You MUST LET GO OF EVERYTHING and GIVE IT ALL TO HIM. If you continue to hold onto these things, this stuff, you may be unwilling to allow God to lead you to your new path. When you consider all your time, your energy, all your efforts and sacrifices you put into building yourself and making a life for yourself it is hard to release it to have it all go away. Although you believe you are living the best you can God has so much more He wants to teach you, to give to you. You must LET GO of anything that will come between you and God. His plans for you and your stuff are so much greater than your plans for you if you would only release it all to Him. He's patiently waiting,

God cannot do anything until you allow Him to come in. (Revelations 3:20). You must kick out all the junk that is controlling you, keeping you resistant, keeping Him locked out.

When you let go and let God it does not mean giving up and not caring, to the contrary, you must care, you must care enough to let go. You need to let go of your will and acknowledge only God can meet all your needs. You must claim as your own the incredibly yet somewhat desperate prayer that Jesus prayed. "Father, if you are willing, take this cup from me; yet not my will but Yours be done" - Luke 22:42. You need to let go and let God do what God wills. This submission will lead to peace and joy, even when the way is difficult. "Father, into your hands I commit my spirit."- Luke 23:46. When you begin to feel stressed out, you need to pause and say, "The LORD is my shepherd; I shall not want" Psalm 23.

Make no mistake about it, you are the one who won't allow God to be real in your life. You constantly struggle, you simply won't let God Be God.

What is Reality?
This is What I've Been Asking All Along

For these rules are only shadows of the reality yet to come. And Christ himself is that reality. - Colossians 2:17

You have no doubt in knowing the world in which you live is real. You find it still here in the morning when you rise, realizing you did not simply think or dream it into existence. It was already here waiting for you when you first arrived even from birth.

You can go outside and feel the wind and the dew of the morning on your face and know they are real. You can see the sun by day, the moon and stars by night. You see the lightning and hear the roar of the thunder in the dark clouds above as the rain and snow fall from the sky. You hear the familiar noises of nature and the sounds of human indignation. Without a doubt, you know all these things are real. When you lie down to slumber at night, you do not fear that it will all somehow fall apart or disappear while you sleep. In the morning, you gain your footing planting your feet on the solid ground beneath you. You look around and enjoy the beauty of the trees, mountains, and valleys all around you and the vast blue sky above all still here just as it was when you closed your eyes the night before. Through hearing, seeing, smelling, tasting, touching and feeling you behold your world your reality.

Even through your finite explanation, you believe God is real.

Unfortunately, He is as real as you define Him to be. You cannot begin to fathom that even a worshipping heart does not and cannot create an Object. Your heart is designed for an endless search and can only find the source of its exploration when it is awakened from a decaying moral sleep through regeneration that is given only by God. All of your reality is contingent upon Him. The greatest truth is God. Through objective existence independent of, and apart from any philosophies you may think you have concerning Him. He created your dependent reality that makes up the sum of all created things, including you.

God and the spiritual world are real. Not as you know reality with our limited mind, you can only use our five senses to confirm those images born out of your mind and attempt to attach a perceived reality to them. Conversely just as much as your assurance of the familiar world around you. Spiritual things albeit unfamiliar to your carnal morals through your restricted logical mind are also here all around you, welcoming your attention while challenging your trust. Faith creates nothing; although yet seen it merely acknowledges that which is already.

The problem is you have been conceived and cultivated in a very visible but fallen world. Your mind has been conditioned to think only of this physical existence as reality casting continual shadows of doubt on even the possibility of any other reality existing. However due to your limited understanding you do not refute the existence of the spiritual world, yet with that same understanding, you have your doubts that it holds the same reality as you through your own definition perceive real.

This world you live in constantly imposes on you demanding 100 % of all your senses, 100 % of the time from cradle to grave. This temporal world known only as your reality has no desire to appeal to your faith. You are continually and relentlessly under attack as the world frequently strong-arms your senses tangibly portraying itself as genuine and absolute. These tactics have succeeded in clogging the filters of your heart, blinding your inner man making it impossible through convoluted pollution for the other reality to freely flow through already clogged arteries of your cardiovascular system. You are being forced daily deeper and deeper into a dark mundane form of existence. One that only amounts to a temporary space of perpetual nocturnal delight so you cannot see that other reality that is the Kingdom of God that exists within you and all around you. The curse bestowed upon you as an inheritance due to your defiance of thought, instead of acceptance of the faith of your unseen reality, the faith that was initially given to you that breeds belief in what is.

There is a reality that lies within all of us, and if allowed can conquer the confusion that exists only in our minds. A mind easily swayed by the inability to see clearly through your natural alienated heart that is held captive being trapped by your underdeveloped eyes that seem only to address the constant invasive attack of visible things. You must consciously shift your concentration from the seen to the unseen, although unseen it is not an unknown for the vast invisible Reality, God.

If you truly want to follow God, you must seek to be other-worldly. But you must avoid the common fault of pushing the "other world" into the future. It does not exist somewhere in the future, as a place that should be treated as a separate yet planned vacation or even futuristic apparition, but very near as to be present in the here and now. It parallels your very familiar physical world, and the doors between the two worlds are open." Our soul has eyes to see and ears to hear. Although they have grown frail from lack of use, with the life-giving touch of Christ they are made alive, therefore, are more than capable of the sharpest sight and most sensitive hearing.

As you focus on God, the things of the spirit will take shape before your inner eyes. Then your obedience to the word of Christ will bring an inward revelation of the Godhead (John 14:21-23). A new God-consciousness will grab you, and you will begin to taste, hear and inwardly feel the God, who is your All.

Live in His Moment
I'm Too Busy Trying to Live in My Own

Take delight in the Lord, and he will give you the desires of your heart. -
Psalm 37:4

Many people never actually manage to enjoy their lives. They spend day after day just going through the motions, hoping things will get better. It's often a pivotal and life-changing moment that leaves you re-evaluating the important things in life, the things you often otherwise take for granted. You know your health, your family, the grass, a beautiful sunset, a glorious sunrise, or the stars at night. Let's not forget the fact that you even opened your eyes at all to yet another beautiful day of life. The truth is many of us spend our lives trying to win it. Living as if life were a game of sorts, competition. Just who, or what, is it that you believe you are racing, what is it that you are trying so hard to beat the next person at doing.

Too often we get so caught up in our busy lives that we tend to forget just how important it is to live unpretentiously and experience each and every moment in its simplicity. Instead, we live for the big things, the exciting times, instead of always appreciating the little things. Most people are too busy planning that special trip, trying to get that big job promotion, always searching, planning, or even waiting for the next Big Thing. Sure it's great to have aspirations and dreams, however, we should also be careful to remember that the day, hour, or the minute is never promised. By living in the now.

By not taking life for granted, by making each and every moment of the day the best it can be. You can have a better life experience. You will be happy, healthy, victorious, and the overcoming conqueror God created you to be!

Life is quickly and quietly passing you leaving you behind, while you're preparing to live, life is happening all around you. Unfortunately, you are too busy planning and making a living rather than taking the time to live life and actually see it. Like the time, Jesus commended Mary for "choosing the better part." In simple terms, Mary's desire to be near her Lord listening to His every word was far more beneficial than running herself ragged with preparations for a meal as her sister Martha was doing. Although both were doing what each felt to be important and beneficial. By Jesus saying Mary had "chosen the better part." He was saying for those whose priority in life is Christ, the knowledge of Him, and nearness to Him have selected what will last through eternity. Things such as the "gold, silver and costly stones" referred to in 1 Corinthians 3:11-12. When you focus on Christ, He becomes your greatest passion and your tendency to self-absorption with the things of life quickly dim and fade.

If you were completely honest with yourself either now or in your past, you would admit you view life like this never ending ever winding road that you are guaranteed to wake up happy and healthy every tomorrow. Although you are very much aware one day, that morning just will not arrive for you in this life. Even the wealthiest, most successful person on earth will eventually age, sicken, and die, and all the wealth in the world cannot prevent it, nor can the fortune be transferred into the next life. For the Christian, however, life here, can always be good. Consider this, you know you already have the victory, you also know all the ways you will experience difficulties in this life. John 16:33 says "These things I have spoken unto you, that in me, ye might have peace. In the world ye shall have tribulation: but be of good cheer; I have overcome the world." But it doesn't stop there you have everything you need to withstand and in some cases defend the attacks in this life. You have the full game plan and are fully equipped to handle any and everything that comes your way. Besides, remember you are already victorious. 1 Corinthians 15:57 – "But thanks be to God, which giveth us the victory through our Lord Jesus Christ."

While it is possible to enjoy living your life now, no matter how good it is, no matter how good it gets, it is nothing compared to the life that awaits you with Him. Some of the divine glories of heaven are described as eternal life, righteousness, joy, peace, perfection. To live eternally in God's presence, to experience the fullness of Christ and enjoy His glorious companionship, your rewards, and all else God has planned is the Christian's heavenly inheritance 1 Peter 1:3-5. The glories of Heaven cause even the best life on earth to pale in comparison. When you know Jesus Christ as your Savior, your best life awaits you with Him. In Him you will spend eternity in joy and bliss, enjoying a life that is better than the "best" life you could ever imagine and it all can begin right now, today, what are you waiting for, your eternity awaits.

Make Your Life Real Today
My Life Is as Real as It Gets

"I am the true vine, and my Father is the gardener." - John 15:1

Sometime after the late 1960s, Eugene Booker McDaniels a singer-songwriter wrote a song titled, "Compared to What" later it became a very famous hit song. A portion of the lyrics goes a little like this "Church on Sunday, sleep, and nod. Tryin' to duck the wrath of God. Preacher's fillin' us with fright, They all tryin' to teach us what they think is right, They really got to be some kind of nut, Tryin' to make it real — compared to what?

Have you ever wondered just as Eugene McDaniels did what you are comparing life to? Have you ever considered your human senses could be deceiving you. Maybe it is your very existence that is nothing more than a delusional state of consciousness, and reality as you know it, could it merely be an Illusion, maybe we are all just trying to make it real but compared to what? We can all agree human senses are fallible. Consider what we think we perceive is filtered and processed through our minds to construct a pragmatic view of the world. Science often describes reality as "the state of things as they exist". One simple interpretation of this very broad definition is this: reality is everything we observe to be real. Albert Einstein once said, "Reality is merely an illusion, albeit a very persistent one"

As Einstein suggested, is every form of reality only an illusion? Is nothing real?

The disciples might have pondered the very same question, after all, they were already living in the very real world, doing real work, having a real life, but real compared to what. Only in our virtual world could we even imagine a person walking on water as Jesus did, as Peter did. Certainly not in our current state of what we consider reality it goes against all of our current laws of physics. Jesus assures his closest followers in John 15:1" I am the True Vine" in other words I am as real as it gets. Jesus wanted his followers to know that even though we cannot see God, we are as closely connected with Him to God, as the branches of a vine are connected with its stem. Jesus emphatically underscored His point even more saying, "Without Me, you can do nothing." That is no thoughtless generality or careless smile. It is an absolute, stark reality. No believer can be anything or achieve anything of spiritual value independently of Jesus. For this reason, we must 'abide' in Him, remaining attached to the source of all spiritual life.

What we have now if we could only receive and accept it, and also in the future with God, in and through Jesus is our real life. Like Peter, we get distracted from what is real, walking on water in his case. In our case, it may be any storm of life where we only see the troubled waves of our life around us. The tides of disappointment, death, destruction, and the riptides of despair, heartaches, and pain it seems the waves of life just as the tides never stop coming in. We tend only to believe what we can physically see and feel in this world. However, are the things of this world more real than the promises of God? The Bible has many bold claims that seem to go against the laws of nature, eternal life with an infinite God after death in this finite life to name just one.

It would serve us well to remember, God is not subject to the laws of nature. He established all of nature and its laws. They are subject to Him. We need to get our focus off the "why, what, when, and how" in this life and put our focus on the "Who." Our spiritual life with Jesus in God is the "real" life God wants us to place our attention. We need to make this life genuine by comparing everything we do, say, and feel to Him.

The apostle Paul reminds us in Colossians 3:3, "For ye are dead, and your life is hidden with Christ in God." It is hidden from our physical eyes. We may not see, feel or touch it right now; in this what we consider the natural realm. However, we must believe God when He says it is real. Although it does not mean the house you live in or any other physical property you have only an illusion—it is as real as you make it. However, there will come a season when it will all pass away. It is time to start living and enjoying our "real" life in Jesus NOW. We honor God when we take our focus off the things of this corruptible world and put it solely on Him, where it belongs. Let us make it "Our Life in Him "real knowing there is no comparison.

Bibliography

Does God Exist?
Psalm 19:1-4
Ecclesiastes 3:11
Romans 1:20
Psalm 14:1
Hebrews 11:6
John 20:29

I Want to Meet God
John 14:7-9

Waiting on God
Acts 16:24-26
Isaiah 40:31

Frustrated with God
Psalm 18:30
Isaiah 26:3
Jonah 1:1-3
Acts 26:14
1 Peter 5:7

What's My Fault?
Mark 1:23
Acts 19:12-13
Luke 13:11
Mark 9:25
James 1:4
Romans 3:10-23
Galatians 5:19-21
1 Corinthians 10:13
1 John 4:4
Matthew 4:1-11
James 4:7

Romans 7:24-25
1 John 5:3-5
1 John 4:4
2 Peter 1:3
Romans 7:20

The Struggle Continues
James 4:7
Ephesians 6:12
Ephesians 5:22-25
1 Peter 5:5
Ephesians 5:21
Philippians 2:3
Romans 8:28-29
Acts 5:29
Acts 5:41

What Did You Call Me?
1 Peter 2:9
John 1:12
Galatians 3:26
1 John 3:10
Colossians 2:10
Colossians 2:6
Colossians 2:7

Taking The Next Step
Joshua 3:1-17
Joshua 3:15
Joshua 3:11
Joshua 3:13-16
Exodus 14:15-16
Isiah 43:2
Joshua 3:11
Joshua 3:5
Joshua 3:13

Hebrew 11:6

Moving Forward
Philippians 3:13-14
Luke 9:62
Philippians 3:13
1 Tim. 1:13
Hebrew 10:17
Hebrew 12: 1
2 Corinthians 11:23-28
2 Corinthians 12:11
2 Tim. 2:6-8
Proverbs 4:18

Days Ahead

John 21:12-13

Learning to Trust God – I Don't Trust Easily
Proverbs 3:5, 6

A Wise Decision
Deuteronomy 30:19
James 1:5
John 14:6

Discover Your Life
John 3:16–18
Acts 10:43
Romans 10:9
2 Corinthians 5:21
John 1:12
Acts 2:21
Colossians 3:3
Romans 6:2, 5
Galatians 6:14

Galatians 2:20
John 17:3
Philippians 3:10
1 John 2:27
Matthew 15:8
Mark 7:6
Matthew 7:22
Matthew 22:37

Mark 12:30
Luke 10:27
Matthew 6:33
Romans 10:9–10
Jeremiah 29:13
Philippians 3:8
Psalm 32:8
Romans 12:1, 2

Balancing Life
Psalms 55:6-8
Psalm 55:22
Matthew 6:33
Ephesians 4:25 – 5:2

Consider Your Focus
James 4:17
2 Cor. 5:17

You Can Say No
Mark 1:35-39
John 17:4
Ephesians 5:15-17
1 Cor. 12:12-31
1 Pet. 4:10-11

A New Life to Share

Acts 20:24

Worship My Way
Jeremiah 2:13

Proverbs 12:15

Hebrews 13:15

Galatians 1:10

Matthew 10:37

Let Go
Matthew 16:24
Revelations 3:20
Luke 22:42
Luke 23:46
Psalm 23

Rooted in Reality
John 14:21-23

Live in His Moment
1 Corinthians 3:11-12
John 16:33
1 Corinthians 15:57
1 Peter 1:3-5

Make Your Life Real Today
John 15:1
Colossians 3:3